1 2 3 4 5 6 7 8 9 10 20 30

FROM ONE
TO
ONE HUNDRED

Teri Sloat

40 50 60 70 80 90 100

SCHOLASTIC INC.

New York   Toronto   London   Auckland   Sydney

To Rebecca,
whom I can always count on

one

You can find as many of these objects in the picture as the number on the page.

two

2

three

four

4

five

5

six

Signpost text in illustration:

OASIS 7 MI.
MARKET 7 MI.
7 MI. DUNES
7 MI. PYRAMIDS
7 MI. CAMP
7 MI. STABLES
7 MI. POST OFFICE

seven

7

eight

8

nine

ten

10

twenty

20

thirty

30

forty

40

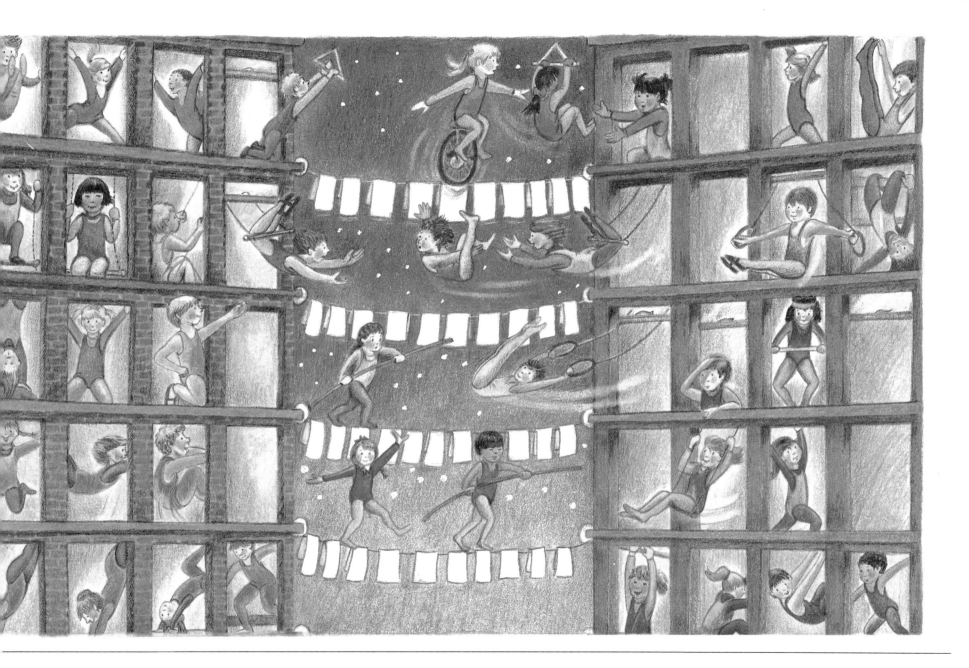

fifty

50

sixty

 60

seventy

70

eighty

80

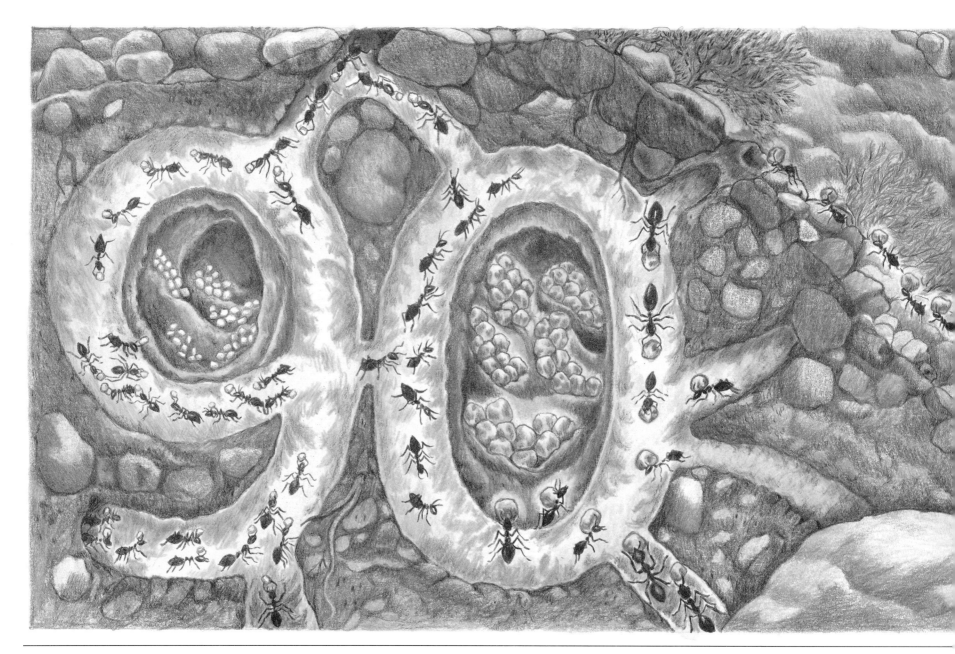

ninety

one hundred

100

1 2 3 4 5 6 7 8 9 10 20 30

Copyright © 1991 by Teri Sloat.
All rights reserved.
Published by Scholastic Inc., 555 Broadway, New York, NY 10012,
by arrangement with Dutton Children's Books,
a division of Penguin Books USA Inc.
Designer: Riki Levinson.
Printed in the U.S.A.
ISBN 0-590-50923-3

1 2 3 4 5 6 7 8 9 10   08   01 00 99 98 97 96 95

40 50 60 70 80 90 100